It's OK I love you I'm with you today. It's OK I love you I'm with you today. It's OK I love you I'm with you today. It's OK I love you I'm with you today. It's OK I love you I'm with you today. It's OK I love you I'm with you today. It's OK I love you I'm with you today. It's OK I love you I'm with you today. It's OK I love you I'm with you today. It's OK I love you I'm with you today. It's OK I love you I'm with you today. It's OK I love you I'm with you today. It's OK I love you I'm with you today. It's OK I love you I'm with you today. It's OK I love you I'm with you today. It's OK I love you I'm with you today. It's OK I love you I'm with you today. It's OK I love you I'm with you today. It's OK I love you I'm with you today. It's OK I love you I'm with you today.

bala kids

An imprint of Shambhala Publications, Inc.
2129 13th Street
Boulder, Colorado 80302
www.shambhala.com

Cover art by Sandra Eide
Design by Kara Plikaitis

9 8 7 6 5 4 3 2

Printed in Malaysia

Shambhala Publications makes every effort to print on acid-free, recycled paper.
Bala Kids is distributed worldwide by Penguin Random House, Inc., and its subsidiaries.

Library of Congress Cataloging-in-Publication Data

Names: O'Leary, Wendy, author. | Eide, Sandra, illustrator.
Title: It's ok: being kind to yourself when things feel hard / Wendy O'Leary; illustrated by Sandra Eide.
Other titles: It is ok
Description: Boulder, Colorado: Shambhala, [2023] | Audience: Ages 3-7 | Audience: Grades K-1
Identifiers: LCCN 2021054663 | ISBN 9781645470953 (hardcover)
Subjects: LCSH: Self-acceptance—Juvenile literature. | Compassion—Juvenile literature. | Mindfulness (Psychology)—Juvenile literature.
Classification: LCC BF575.S37 O434 2023 | DDC 158.1—dc23/eng/20220125
LC record available at https://lccn.loc.gov/2021054663

It's OK

Being Kind to Yourself When Things Feel Hard

Wendy O'Leary

Illustrated by Sandra Eide

Sometimes things don't go the way I want.

I feel sad, and it is hard.

Then I remember
that everyone feels sad sometimes.

I put my hand on my heart, and here's what I say:

It's OK — I love you.

I'm with you today.

Sometimes I make a mistake.
I feel really bad. . . .

Then I remember that everyone feels bad sometimes.

I put my hand on my heart, and here's what I say:

It's OK—I love you.
I'm with you today.

Sometimes I have to do something I don't want to do.
I feel really angry. . . .
Then I remember that everyone feels angry sometimes.

I put my hand on my heart, and here's what I say:

It's OK — I love you. I'm with you today.

Sometimes I can't do something no matter how hard I try.
I feel frustrated. . . .
Then I remember that everyone feels frustrated sometimes.

I put my hand on my heart, and here's what I say:

It's OK — I love you. I'm with you today.

Sometimes my fun plans get canceled.
I feel so disappointed. . . .

Then I remember that everyone feels disappointed sometimes.

I put my hand on my heart, and here's what I say:

It's OK—I love you.
I'm with you today.

Sometimes I am not included.
I feel so hurt. . . .

Then I remember that everyone feels hurt sometimes.

I put my hand on my heart, and here's what I say:

It's OK — I love you.

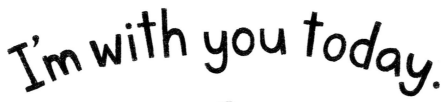

I'm with you today.

Sometimes I think something bad might happen.
I feel so worried. . . .
Then I remember that everyone feels worried sometimes.

I put my hand on my heart, and here's what I say:

It's OK—I love you. I'm with you today.

Sometimes I think I'm just not special.
I feel like I'm not good enough. . . .

Then I remember that everyone feels not good enough sometimes.

I put my hand on my heart, and here's what I say:

It's OK—I love you.

I'm with you today.

Be your own friend by trying some of these exercises.

Use This Book

When something is hard, remind yourself to use the words we learned in this book.

I put my hand on my heart, and here's what I say:
"It's OK—I love you. I'm with you today."

Kind Touch

Put your hand on your heart. How does that feel?

Put your hand on your cheek. How does that feel?

Hold your own hand. How does that feel?

Experiment with different ways to give yourself a kind touch!

Kind Talk

Imagine a time when you have felt bad or another feeling in this book.

What would a friend say to you if you were feeling this way?

What would you say to someone you love who was feeling this way?

Can you come up with one kind thing you could say to yourself when things are hard?

Kind Voice

Say one kind thing to yourself using different voices.
Try using an angry voice, a sad voice, a silly voice.
Then try using a kind and caring voice.
How do you feel when you talk
to yourself in these voices?
Say a nice thing to yourself
using a kind voice.

Kind Body

Look in a mirror and say one kind thing to yourself while watching your body.

Try it with an angry body, a sad body, a silly body. Then try it with a kind and caring body.

How do you feel?

Look in the mirror and say a nice thing to yourself with a kind voice and a kind body.

Noodles

Lie down and make your body tight like you are a package of noodles before being cooked. Hold your body really tight like that, and count to five. Then imagine the noodles when they are all cooked. Pretend to be the cooked noodles, and let your body get soft and loose. Count to five.

Hugging Breath

Put your arms out wide on each side as you breathe in, then wrap your arms around yourself in a hug as you breathe out. Try three to five hugging breaths.

Tree Time

Stand up tall like a tree and feel your feet on the ground. Imagine that you are a tree and your feet have roots connecting you to the earth. Now lean to one side and imagine that just one leg is the trunk of the tree, then switch to the other side. Do this a few times before coming back to having both feet be the base of your solid tree trunk.

Now lift your arms like branches, but keep your feet, legs, and body like the trunk of the tree, perfectly still. You can even let the branches move, but don't forget that your trunk is attached to the ground and is strong, solid, and still.

Self-Compassion Is Great for Grown-ups Too!

This book was inspired by the work of three leading experts and authors in the field of self-compassion: Christopher Germer, PhD, clinical psychologist; Kristin Neff, PhD, pioneering self-compassion researcher and co-developer, with Dr. Germer, of the Mindful Self Compassion Program; and clinical psychologist and professor Shauna Shapiro, PhD.

I have found practices of self-compassion to be vital in my own life. Any understanding of these teachings and their benefits will support you in sharing them with the children in your life.

Afterword

This wonderful book teaches us the essence of self-compassion in the easiest possible way.

Self-compassion is an inner resource we all have, but it usually remains untapped. We now know that self-compassion can make us happier, more emotionally resilient, more compassionate toward others, and even improve physical health. Sadly, most of us are far less compassionate with ourselves than with others when things go wrong.

How can we become more self-compassionate? When children are raised in a safe, loving environment, they tend to be kinder to themselves. Children internalize how they're treated. However, no matter how wonderful a child's upbringing may be, they are still likely to beat up on themselves when things go wrong.

Happily, this book is the perfect tool to teach young children to be kind to themselves in those moments. Young children take to it rather easily, as if it's the most natural thing in the world. As children age and receive cultural messages against caring for themselves, it becomes more elusive. *It's OK* gives children *permission* to use self-love as a coping tool during challenging times. It really is a humble enterprise—we're just including ourselves in the circle of our compassion.

Most importantly, this sweet book shows kids how simple self-compassion can be. The essence of the practice is perfectly captured in repeated key phrases: "I feel," "I remember that *everyone* feels," and "I put my hand on my heart." That's the magic of these three ingredients—mindfulness, common humanity, and self-kindness (as originally formulated by the psychologist Kristin Neff).

We all want to protect our children from emotional distress. Unfortunately, hardship is part of the human condition. Parental love and support are essential for managing difficult emotions in young children, but eventually each person needs to be able to love and support themselves. This book will help you plant seeds of self-compassion in the hearts of your children that will nourish them for a lifetime.

CHRISTOPHER GERMER, PHD

Lecturer on Psychiatry, Harvard Medical School
Author, *The Mindful Path of Self-Compassion*

I love you. I'm with you today. It's OK I love you I'm with you to
ith you today. It's OK I love you. I'm with you today. It's OK I lo
I love you. I'm with you today. It's OK I love you I'm with you to
ith you today. It's OK I love you I'm with you today. It's OK I lo
I love you I'm with you today. It's OK I love you I'm with you to
ith you today. It's OK I love you I'm with you today. It's OK I lo
I love you I'm with you today. It's OK I love you I'm with you to
ith you today. It's OK I love you I'm with you today. It's OK I lo
I love you I'm with you today. It's OK I love you I'm with you to
ith you today. It's OK I love you I'm with you today. It's OK I lo
I love you I'm with you today. It's OK I love you I'm with you to
ith you today. It's OK I love you I'm with you today. It's OK I lo
I love you I'm with you today. It's OK I love you I'm with you to
ith you today. It's OK I love you I'm with you today. It's OK I lo
I love you I'm with you today. It's OK I love you I'm with you to
ith you today. It's OK I love you I'm with you today. It's OK I lo
I love you I'm with you today. It's OK I love you I'm with you to
ith you today. It's OK I love you I'm with you today. It's OK I lo